NOW WE ARE SIXTY

by

FELICITY HOFFECKER

Art by VIRGINIA BATES

TWO BYTES PUBLISHING, LTD.
1998

DEDICATION

FOR MY GRANDSONS -
IAN, JIM, JEFF AND ADAM

Table of Contents

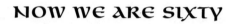

NOW WE ARE SIXTY

So They Say

They say you are as old as you feel,
*   GREAT!*
So then why do people help me into chairs
*   and treat me as if I'm some old geezer?*
And why don't the boys whistle at me
*   As I walk down the street?*

If I am old as I feel
*   Why am I relegated to an armchair when everyone else is dancing?*
I feel the same way I did when I was sixteen,
*   But no one seems to realize it.*

Cracking Up

The chimney sweep came to my house today to clean out the fireplace and its overpinnings.

"You've got a lot of holes in the chimney up above outside," he informed me, as he climbed down the ladder from the roof."

"What should I do about them?" I asked.

"Well, you should really have the whole thing pulled down and rebuilt," he told me as he wiped his sooty hands on his shirt.

"How much would that cost?" I enquired apprehensively.

"Oh, about a thousand dollars," he hazarded.

This conversation reminded me of one I had had about a week ago when the man came to clean my furnace for the winter.

That's really a very old-fashioned furnace," he said, as he packed up his tools to leave. "You really should have a new one put in as soon as possible."

"How much would a new one cost?" I asked him.

"Oh, about twenty-five hundred," he replied.

This is rapidly becoming the tenor of my life. It seems that everything I have is old and worn and would cost thousands to replace. Whatever happened to that old Puritan ethic of use it up, wear it out, make it do?

The garage people look askance at my '84 Toyota and wonder aloud if it will last through another winter. The mowing machine repair man shakes his head as he unloads my machine from my car. The dishwasher repair man asks me in wonderment how long I have had my dishwasher and is amazed visibly that it still continues to function.

Workmen hired to attend to other machines in the house tell me they thought such models were not being made anymore and that it would be impossible to come by any of the parts for repair.

"Now I am overdue for a physical at my doctor's, and I am afraid to go near him. I know so well what he is going to say: "This model went out of date years ago. I'd advise you to turn it in as soon as possible before it breaks down completely."

And adding, "And it will cost you about two thousand dollars."

Homage to Hot Water

Most of the younger generation in America – the one before that, too, probably – have never known a life bereft of a constant supply of hot water. But, for some of us who are older and who have lived in a variety of old houses without that benefit, the gorgeous hot steamy gush that comes forth by the simple procedure of turning a knob is still one of the greatest blessings of modern life.

For our forefathers who first turned that knob, it must have seemed miraculous. Early mornings of going out to the pump or well to fill a bucket are, thank god, long gone by.

But in my childhood, I stayed in old country houses that still provided wash basin and slop jar behind discreet bedroom screens. Sometimes we were lucky. The water in the jugs was hot and was carried up there by faithful servants and later emptied out by them.

In Australia, at a country home where we once lived, bath water was headed in a tall brass cylinder at the front end of the tub. The fire in the cylinder was fed with twigs from the nearby Eucalyptus trees, and the blue smoke emerging from its ventilator was redolent with their wonderful, unforgettable aroma, adding much to the bath experience itself.

Large country houses in which I stayed in chilly England had large chilly bathtubs to match – so large and chilly that the small stream of hot water trickling from their taps was cold long before it had covered a few inches of tub. Then, too, there were always the signs on the bulletin boards of hotels and flats that told us that there would be no hot water after four o'clock.

In the country house in Virginia where I grew up, there was hot water readily available – in winter, when the furnace was noisily knocking itself out heating the house as well as the water pipes. In summer, there was none. None, that is unless you wanted to spend some hot afternoon gathering twigs and battling with the contrariness of a small black stove in the basement. Too often I spent my afternoon hours in this occupation, only to emerge black and perspiring into a bathtub whose tap produced only a cold trickle. *The fire had gone out.*

My father, having been raised in proper British school-boy fashion, was proud of the fact that he took a cold bath every morning of his life. Like caning, a staple of the education system of the day, he felt it made a man of you, showed you were of *The Proper Stuff*. Years later, I read many autobiographies of British writers who claimed that fighting in the trenches in 1914-1918 was not really that bad after you had undergone life in a British boarding school.

My former husband who served as a medical officer in the next war and demanded more of the comforts of life, once decided while encamped somewhere in France that what he wanted more than anything was the experience of a hot bath. Thus, he wrote to me afterwards, he spent an afternoon collecting firewood, hunting up a large vessel to place over it, filling the basin with sufficient water and waiting for it to heat. It took most of his day and all his energies, creative as well as physical. But the final results were, he reported, most satisfactory.

Falling Leaves and Losing Battles

My late husband and I were both un-mechanical. I had to take Physics three times in college before I was able to pass it, and then I think they just let me through rather than face me again. I was never able to understand what makes motors run. My husband was little better. He didn't even drive a car.

Thus, it was something of a shock to our sensibilities when we produced two sons who could say the word "truck" before they could even mouth "Mama" or "Daddy", and before reaching the age of six, knew the types of every truck on the road. Fifty cents meant to them the chance to buy another Matchbox model, more brought visions of Dinky Toy, the windowsills of their room lined with these minute vehicles. Any attempts by their parents to introduce them to the delights of Peter Rabbit or Mrs. Tiggywinkle, were passed over for "The Wonderful World of Trucks" or "Rackety Boom".

So it should have come as no surprise to me when, years later, my younger son's small twin boys were equally avid for the same trucks. Fairy tales and Winnie the Pooh left them cold, and walks in Nature's wonderland were only exciting if the wonderland ran alongside a highway. At Christmas one year I noticed that a small toy truck had joined the worshipping animals around my small creche. When we took them to a farm to see baby animals, their interest was quickly caught by the truck parked there that had brought in the hay.

I showed them around my garden, holding forth on the wonders of Nature, had them plant seeds and watch the miracle of growth, and finally seemed to be making headway.

Especially when, one night, I saw them sitting on my bed and gazing out of the window at the line of trees that stand between my view and I-95.

"Soon the leaves will turn yellow and red," murmured one of them dreamily to his brother.

"And they will fall from the trees," commented the other one thought-fully...and then added triumphantly with great satisfaction.

"And then we'll be able to see the trucks on the highway!"

Saturday

Saturday morning had a very special aura for me when I was a child in Australia. I could feel it even as I was waking up. I would lie in bed, alternately squinting my eyes to see the wallpaper in the hall in different ways through the slats of my bed and the waving fronds of bamboo against the blue sky outside the window. The sky was almost always blue. After all, it was Australia. And it was Saturday, SATURDAY, SATURDAY!...

Saturday was so perfect. Weekdays were filled with school which I hated, and Sundays meant church and, often enough, going out to tea somewhere, being chucked under the chin and told how tall I was getting. There were long hours of suffocating boredom while grown-ups talked and laughed about absolutely nothing. Sunday night meant homework I had never done all weekend, and the heavy gloom of five school days loomed ahead.

But Saturday...there was nothing to mar it. First, getting up and getting dressed – not in the hated school uniform with the heavy serge tunic, the confining white blouse and school tie, the dreadful "liberty bodice" that supplied the garters to hold up the darned grey woolen stockings. Saturday meant dressing in pretty flowered dresses, socks and sandals, all of which could be put on in a matter of minutes.

Breakfast in the dining room found Father, as usual, behind the newspaper and Mother, behind the teapot. When she was not there, I have been told, I sat down and ate my breakfast in a civilized fashion, watching the milk flowing on the mountain of porridge on my Felix the Cat plate. But when she was there, I knew I could get the attention I craved, I tossed my fried egg about the plate and threw my toast at the wall in temperamental fits. If no one was there, I often just went to the window and threw the whole plateful outside. It was much simpler. In any case, I could hardly wait to get through and get down the street to spend my pocket money.

They say a fool and his money are soon parted, and if so, I was indeed a fool, because my money never rested a moment in my eager grasp. How different was my sister, five years older, who always put hers, virtuously, into her bank, saying she was "saving" though she never specified for what. It was the same with toys. When we each received a Christmas present, say a new paint box from our artist uncle, or a doll, I took mine out and played with it relentlessly until it was used up,

worn out or broken, but my sister put hers away "for good".

The shelf in her cupboard was piled high with things she had put away "for good", including two sugar columns from our aunt's wedding cake. Long ago I had licked them both hollow. But vice has its own reward. When we left Australia some years later, all of them had to be given away – *unused*.

As soon as breakfast was disposed of, I was on my way down the street, banging against each fencepost as I skipped my way along, leaving hard peppermints in the spaces between them. I always checked, on my way back, to see if anyone had discovered these treasures. I was amazed that no one had snatched up the handful of dirty white morsels lodged there. Then, on past Laventree Road, (which we called Lavatory Road) and down Manningtree Road, past our school, Stratherne Presbyterian Girls' Grammar School. On the plaque, the name was written: "Stratherne P.G.G.S." Naturally, someone had inserted an "*I*" between the "P" and "G".

Crossing the main thoroughfare, Power Street, I came to the line of shops. There was the draper with his store full of wonderful smells of fresh fabrics, his collection of spools, thimbles and his big shears. Sometimes I went in there to buy a quarter of a yard of material for dolls' clothes. There was the grocer with his sawdust covered floor, his infinite shelves filled with various sizes of colored cans and bottles. The butcher came next. I avoided looking at the ghastly row of bleeding carcasses hanging from his hooks and went on by the florist, stopping only to sniff the big bunches of eucalyptus branches, smoky grey and blue, outside on the pavement.

Best of all were the stationery store and the sweet shop. In the former I could bury my nose in the rubbers (erasers) and punch their pungent spongy interiors, sniff the wonderful odor of newsprint, gaze with excitement at the rows of brilliant comics on display. There was Playtime, Playbox, Rainbow and Tiger Tim.

Almost all of them contained stories about boys' or girls' schools, the pupils all being animals dressed in clothes. Chick's Own was a comic for little kids. All of them contained contests in which one competed for rare prizes, sending in entries to Uncle Dick or Uncle Dan in Fleet Street. Alas...Fleet Street was in London, the other side of the world, and the entry date was over before the comics even arrived in Australia. But then, all of our pencils and books carried that stamp, "Made In Britain". I usually bought a comic and moved on to the sweet shop where I spent much time making decisions between gelatin hats, licorice whips, humbugs and all-day suckers.

My pockets heavy with loot and my face misshapen with jaw breakers, I went happily home to play or read with my new treasures. My father had built us a two-story house in the garden in which to play, but my sister's idea of playing in it was *cleaning* it. I carefully eschewed that kind of entertainment and went, instead, to the swing under the pear tree where I could rock, hum and eat in peace. The pear tree, I was convinced, contained the entrance to fairyland, and I was always hunting for the doorway. I had written countless letters to the fairies, always on pink paper and hidden them in flowers, but they had never cared to reveal themselves to me. One night I had come out the back door and actually seen a shining silver doorway in the pear tree, lit up by moonlight. I was overcome with excitement, feeling that – at last – it had come to be, and I hurried across the lawn on tiptoes in case it disappeared before I got there. It turned out to be a kerosene tin someone had left outside.

Often enough, we were called to shell peas. I seem to have devoted the best years of my life to shelling peas. As a result, I take great delight in buying packages of frozen peas. My sister, Peg, and I sat on the back steps and talked as we shelled. There were the fat pods, bursting with round solid peas, the thin ones with mere slivers and the surprise ones which turned out to be far more fully or far less fully endowed with what one had been led to suspect. Sometimes we dropped in a piece of shell for diversion, to see who would be the *lucky* one to get it at the table.

Mid-day dinner was always a hot one, despite the climate. British families did not fool around with light lunches, and we sat down to hot or cold roast meat, potatoes and...

peas! The meal was followed by stewed fruit and custard or a large suet pudding drowning in treacle.

In the afternoon Peg and I spread out all our paper dolls on the carpet to play. We had many families, and they had, of course, many children. Peg drew them all, and when we thought a year had elapsed, she drew all the children one size larger. Since drawing boys and men was almost impossible, we sent the former off "to boarding school" and the latter "to work" and eliminated that problem. But Peg claimed that drawing them all ruined her talent, and from then on, all the people she drew were stiff figures, their arms by their sides, dressed in underwear.

My mother had no patience with paper dolls. Why were we not out in the good fresh air? Obviously, because the good fresh air blew all our paperdolls away. She had been raised in Ireland where the air was constantly drenched with rain so she appreciated sunshine. After a few summers in Ireland, I could see her point. Playing outside there meant having to run under the trees every few minutes to avoid showers. But, here we had sun with the good fresh air, so we dutifully packed up our paper dolls, not without protests, and trooped outside.

Once there we spread a blanket under one of the apple trees and while I lay on my stomach happily drawing and coloring pictures, my sister read aloud to me, usually from L. M. Montgomery. Earlier, it had been fairytales; later, it would be Dickens, but at this stage we revelled together in the adventure of *Anne of Green Gables* and that remote and romantic part of the world, Prince Edward Island, in Canada, our fellow colony. Mrs. Montgomery had written some twenty books, and we had them all. When we had read through them, we began at the beginning all over again. Some Australian writers, such as Mary Grant Bruce and Ethel Turner, wrote books about the outback, Australian books about life on sheep stations. We liked them a lot, but we preferred L. M. Montgomery.

The late afternoon began to wane, the nice fresh air began to cool, and we went in to tea. Afterwards, I would roam about the garden, play with the cat, sing songs to myself, swing on the apple tree, and generally enjoy being idle until supper and bed. My parents were often going out and made a cameo appearance in evening dress in our doorway, my father handsome in tails and "looking like Clive Brooks". Or, they entertained guests, and the dining room table was spread with dainty sandwiches wrapped in damp linen napkins. Early the next morning we would scoop up handfuls of these morsels to eat in bed as we read.

If our parents were home, they might come in and tell us stories. Father's adventures were of growing up in a gold-mining town in the country; mother's stories were rather gruesome fairy tales dredged up from her Gaelic imagination.

And so Saturday ended. Lying in bed, I could see the moon above the bamboo outside the window; squinting my eyes, the wallpaper. Tomorrow was church and the big Sunday dinner of roast lamb and the inevitable *peas*. A Sunday outing meant a long, dull walk through an art gallery until one's head ached from the elastic chin strap under one's hat, or the adult tea aforementioned. I lay in bed and felt sad and wistful.

Next weekend seemed to be far, far away. Saturday was over.

To Market, To Market

My earliest memories of going to the grocery store are those of a large room full of shelves containing boxes and bottles, a beaming clerk and sawdust all over the floor.

My husband once told me that he remembered his mother going out to shop for comestibles in Richmond, Virginia, sitting in her carriage. She did not get out of it either, but sat back giving her orders from its recesses.

Living in England after World War II, I learned to shop the European way, with a basket over my arm. When one bought a pound of potatoes, they were promptly dumped into it. <u>That</u> was at the *greengrocers*.

From there one went to the grocers, the dairy and the fishmonger – this last named having a dubious other meaning in Shakespeare's time. What was particularly fascinating about this stall was the patterns and arrangements he made with his wares, rather like a Japanese gardener with his stones. A row of flounder might decorate the bottom of the display, a fringe of mackerel the top, circles of cod in the center. And in a final burst of artistic exuberance, a spray of greenery sprouting forth from the mouth of the major participant.

To shop in England after the war meant trying to find equivalents or substitutes for items one needed, especially meat. One learned that tuna fish was called "tunny fish", for example. Once in our village store, I came across imitation maple syrup, so good that we toyed with the idea of having cases shipped to us on our return home.

One might suppose, back in the United States, that all grocery stores were much the same everywhere one went. Not so! A visit to the good old A & P in any part of the country can give you a good clue as to the kind of culture a particular region enjoys. For example, the A & P in Key West, Florida, is lined with cans of frijoles negros (a type of black beans) or the one in Georgia with cans of grits. When I lived in Bay Ridge, New York (the Norwegian section of Brooklyn), the local emporium carried large supplies of cod fish cakes and loaves of limpke. Moving to Darien, Connecticut, I was confronted with an aisle dedicated solely to dog food.

As a friend commented, "It's like these quick travel comedies – if this is Tuesday, this must be Belgian.

"If this is dog food, this must be Darien!"

School Picnic

At the time of year when school picnics abound and the beach parking lot is encumbered with big yellow buses, the sands sprinkled with small active bodies, I find myself recalling once more the excitement that this event engendered in my own childhood.

Our school picnic took place in Melbourne, Australia, and on the day of its celebration I woke up and realized suddenly that this was THE DAY. I lay in bed, tingling with excitement, and watched the yellow bamboo outside the nursery window waving in the breeze against the blue sky. I lay there and prayed that it would not rain.

In school, seated on the small wooden chairs drawn up in a circle round our teacher, I squirmed at the discomfort of the bumpy back, carved as it was to show the emu and the kangaroo holding up the arms of Australia between them. I sat and stared out the window at the Australian flag blowing in the wind against the still bright blue sky, and prayed some more. One cloud and the whole event might be called off. "Please, please, God, don't let it rain," I murmured.

At mid-morning, my prayers answered, I lined up with all the other girls from my class, together with some from others, each of us grasping firmly the bags which held bathing suits and towels. Two by two, we were lined up by our teachers to march in crocodile form to the railway station. The train was to take us to one of the many beaches on Port Phillip Bay, a beach called Sandringham. The name of the beach always associated, in my mind, something to do with "sand" and "ham", thus most appropriate for a picnic.

At our destination we spilled rapidly out of the carriage and raced to the shore. A large rock guarded the entrance down a flight of stairs to our paradise. Just seeing the rock was an excitement all of its own – a symbol of freedom from our daily school existence.

We were all longing to get into the water, to exchange our hot, heavy navy blue tunics for our woolen bathing suits and baggy caps. But, first, there was lunch – as if anyone wanted to waste time with such trivialities. Sandwiches were handed out to hands already sandy, chewed rapidly despite their grainy texture. Rumors flew. "Did you know Olive Agar ate EIGHT egg sandwiches?"

Then, into suits and into the water to splash and swim, to come out and feel the hot sand underfoot, to collect shells and seaweed, cuttlefish and jellyfish with which to drape castles. To

24

make tunnels, to dig for water. My best friend and I walked along the edge of the water blissfully chatting. A rare opportunity for young school girls growing up in a country with rigid social codes. How different everyone looked out of uniform – even the teachers looked human.

On one particular school picnic I remember, I found myself wandering by an open bathhouse where a group of young people were gathered about a player piano, the great fashion of the day, singing, laughing and talking – the young men with their tops covering their chests and the young women wearing Japanese kimonos (again, the fashion of the day) over their still damp suits with their long hair hanging down their backs. I stood and stared, fascinated. "So that's what it's like being grown-up," I pondered.

The sun continued its descent, and the late afternoon became cooler as we were sent off to change back into hot uniforms, pack "bathing togs" into our bags, and replace on our heads straw hats adorned with school ribbon and badge. "How could a

day pass so quickly?" I agonized as we left "paradise" to ascend the seemingly endless flight of steps to the road, steps over which we had flown so lightly earlier in the day.

The train seemed hot and heavy, no one felt much like talking. Uniforms itched against sandy skin, salt-watered throats were parched. The train ride was endless, and the march back to school was exhausting. We were eager to get home.

Yet, what a day it had been! Over sixty years have passed, and its complete and unalloyed happiness has never faded from memory. I look at young children excitedly coming into the beach entrance at the Cove and know how well how they feel. I wonder, too, if they will remember this particular day – sixty years later.

Conundrum

When I was sixteen and had a date
And had to promise not to stay out late,
I sat at my dresser and checked my supplies –
Pancake for face and mascara for eyes.
I couldn't present myself to the world
If my rouge was crooked and my lashes not curled,
My hair swept up and planted with bows,
Eyebrows plucked and powdered nose.
I was perfectly sure that I would faint
Unless my face was covered with paint.

And yet in the past my skin was clear,
My complexion naturally without peer.
I probably looked better the way I was,
But no one could tell me that of course.

Now with wrinkles and creases too
And needing the make-up I eschew
I laugh at the irony of fate
That ruined my skin for a forgotten
date.

The Unquenchable Flame

The dreams and ideals of youth can be very beautiful and very precious, the more so for the child brought up in a world of books.

My own childhood reading touched on many heroines whose deeds filled me with longing to follow in their footsteps. Grace Darling had set out from her lighthouse home in a storm to row shipwrecked mariners to safety. Joan of Arc had led the French army into battle and victory and had a king crowned by her efforts. And in the Australian countryside where I spent my early years, tales of brave rescues abounded. One in particular that I could never forget, concerned the young girl who, hearing that the dreaded bush fires were racing towards her home across the dry countryside, placed her young siblings in a gully (or ditch) and then lay across them to protect them from the flames.Of course, she was crippled for life, but what heroism!

No such opportunities presented themselves in my life, and as I grew older, no chance arose for me to demonstrate my courage and

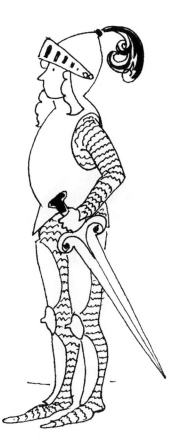

selfless idealism but the flame within me never died. There came a night in Virginia, however, where my family was living during my college years, when I was awakened by the sounds of voices in the driveway below. Some Boy Scouts had inadvertently let a fire of theirs get out of control down in the pine forest near our lake, and friends and neighbors were busy arming themselves with brooms and rakes ready to hurry down there and see that the fire was put out.

I was dressed and out with them in a matter of seconds, my blood racing with excitement. The fire must be held back, subdued, before it reached our house. I tore down through the bushes and trees to where the action was taking place, beating back furiously at the small flames alight in the bushes on the way. I rushed to and fro hacking wildly with my broom, ignoring brambles and rocks in my path. Late in the night when the foe was vanquished, I came home wearily to bed, my arms and legs badly scarred, my hair singed, my heart aglow with heroism.

Next day back at college, some of my friends exclaimed with horror at the sight of my legs – my arms being covered – and I recounted to them the exciting battle I had waged the night before in the forest flames. I described it all in livid color, awaiting their breathless admiration. They, still staring in wonder at my battle-scarred legs, however, only said, "Why didn't you cover them with stockings this morning?"

Not everyone, of course, grew up with Grace Darling and the bushfire heroines of the Australian outback, but for those that did, the zeal for heroism dies hard. In later years, living with my husband and sons in the Connecticut countryside, we were, one afternoon, alerted by a horrendous fire on our neighbor's estate across the road. Their large barn filled with cows and new supplies of hay had suddenly burst into flames. People were racing down our road to witness the conflagration.

I never hesitated. Garbed as I was in a simple cotton housecoat, I was across the road like a flash of lightning. "Did all the cows get out safely?" I demanded of the lady of the house, ready at a moment's notice to dash into the roaring barn and rescue them all single-handed. She stared at me blankly as I quickly asked what I could do before taking off for the barn itself. Nothing apparently, but I hung around for quite a while, just in case.

"I don't know what gets into your mother sometimes," I heard my husband say irritably to my sons as I arrived home, hot and breathless. And sometime later, when some neighboring children inadvertently set the grass afire down by our pond and I called the fire department, the lady across the way came over with all her friends to sit and watch it superciliously and show me, once more, what an ass I had been.

Perhaps I might have had better luck leading an army to victory in France!

Fallen Idols

When I was a small girl, and later when I was growing up, I knew that there were certain people, certain institutions, that were always right. One never for a moment ever questioned the infallibility of the Minister, the Doctor, the Bank, the Headmistress, my Father or my Big Sister, though oddly enough my mother never came under this heading.

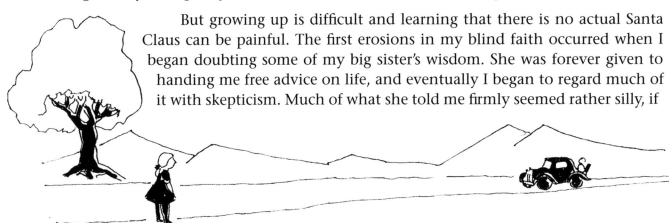

But growing up is difficult and learning that there is no actual Santa Claus can be painful. The first erosions in my blind faith occurred when I began doubting some of my big sister's wisdom. She was forever given to handing me free advice on life, and eventually I began to regard much of it with skepticism. Much of what she told me firmly seemed rather silly, if not downright nonsense. "Never cross a street when a car is coming, even if it is a mile away. This struck me as not making much sense. It seemed then, and still does, the ideal time to make one's way over to the other side.

My father was something else again – the Rhodes scholar, the well-known scientist whom we must never disturb when he was in his study, whose opinions my sister quoted with reverence and whose presence remained formidable until I was almost an adult. But in later years, reading his journals I was taken aback at some of his conclusions. "Do I recommend caning for boys?" he asked. "Yes, I do. It makes a man of them." This was certainly dubious, but so also was his strong belief in a cold bath every morning – also to prove manhood; but more likely it was really because in his youth, hot water was not available easily, if at all. I recalled, too, that he took pride in always eating the fat on meat – doubtless because it is distasteful, therefore character-building. He ate the same breakfast every day of his life – bacon, eggs and cornflakes – and the same lunch (cheese sandwich), and I wonder what his, the Doctor's, cholesterol count must have been when he died at the age of 73. To wonder, too, at all the delights he missed – hot water and delicious food.

Of course, I believed in Doctors. My father was one, and my first husband (his assistant) was one. They always knew best. You took whatever they told you to take without questioning, even shots a doctor gave me during the war, the nature of which I never actually ascertained. I knew that doctors always *know best* and were firmly pictured in my mind by the art of Norman Rockwell. Then, during my husband's long illness, my blood pressure soared, and a Florida doctor put me on a daily sedative, the effects of which were to make me so dull-witted and stupid that for years after

DR. UPRIGHT

I was unable to get a job, or, getting it, was daily taunted by my incompetence. I was kept on the sedative as my depression persisted. A concerned friend asked me what I was taking and told me to get off it fast! I did. I came back to intelligent life once more, but my confidence was shattered.

The fallibility of headmistresses I learned about when I became a teacher and was often astonished by what I saw.

My respect for bankers continued much longer. Since math was never my strong subject, I figured that any mistake in my monthly statement must be my own and adjusted my bank book accordingly. THEN, I got a calculator and began to be more critical. When my bank informed me one month that far from having the $192 in my account that I had come up with, I was actually overdrawn $52. I was thunderstruck. After much backing and filling, it was discovered that I had not counted in a late check of $60, but I was far from overdrawn. The bank was actually **wrong**! Another idol bit the dust.

And ministers...well, so far so good!

That Old Feeling

My school days were spent, along with my sister, at a series of girls' private schools. Our summers were spent at a girls' camp in Vermont. When I attended college, it was at a university that kept the boys on one side of the lake, the girls on the other. Mondays the boys went to chapel, Wednesdays the girls. Fridays was mixed. It was the only day I ever got religion.

Seeing all those boys there in chapel was a truly exciting experience. I had gone to dancing class at one point in my youth and been propelled about the floor by various large-footed oafs steadily chewing Dentyne chewing gum into my hair, but this was something else again. I felt like Miranda in Shakespeare's "Tempest". I wanted to cry out, like her, "Oh, brave new world that has such people in it!"

I have been informed by people who knew me at this stage of my life that I was then "boy crazy" as well as a "late developer". It would have been quite different, they assured me, had I gone to school with boys or had brothers with friends. Seeing them around sooner and more often, I would have become used to the opposite sex and been able to take their presence more calmly.

Nonsense! No one ever gets used to the opposite sex, and that is why they continue to be so exciting.

I have taught in co-educational schools and have been well aware of the vibes going throughout the room by these reputedly used-to-each-other opposite sexes. I have been in a room full of middle-aged women and seen how they all pep up when a man, even somebody's husband, comes through the door. And I have worked in a newspaper office filled with cynical journalists and printers and watched what happened when some blue-eyed miss turned up at the door with her release.

The fact of the matter is that sex continues to titillate wherever it turns up. It is the basis of most plays and almost all novels. It is the big thing in movies and music – ever listen to Wagner's "Tristan and Isolde"? Look at the ads for movies in the paper and on the billboards. Nine out of ten show a couple in impassioned embrace. Look at the travel ads, and you wonder if there is any use going to any of these exotic places without a strong male to clasp in your arms – or vice versa.

My older son became aware of these gender difference while in kindergarten. He came home and told me forlornly that he thought the teacher liked the girls better than the boys. When I asked him why he said it was because the girls wore "those pretty dresses."

He also once confided in me that he was glad he was a boy and not a girl. Fascinated and with great Freudian notions sweeping through my head, I asked the reason. He told me. "'Boy' is easier to spell. I always spell 'girl' as 'Gril'." (I think he still does.)

One of the many delusions held by the young is that once they are married, they will never look at any one else of the opposite sex. The bad part of this attitude is that when they become captivated by someone of that sex, they feel they must get divorced and marry them on the spot. Bad because after that they may well be attracted to still another, and thus begin the old *marry-go-round* machine, never realizing that marriage is something more than attraction and requires loyalty and a memory of what has been shared. Not realizing that just because one is married, one should cease to have eyes in one's head and that a nice-looking person is always a pleasure to contemplate. When you stop enjoying such contemplation, you have really dried up indeed.

Because there IS a difference between the sexes. Men may grow their hair long and women take to wearing pants, but women still do not have to shave every day or men to struggle into panty hose. And it is not only physical. Take a look at couples next time you are in a restaurant. Men sitting together at a table are engaged in a quiet and desultory conversation. Two women, seen at another, are pouring their guts out.

And, as the French say, *"Eh bien pour le petit difference!"*

Yours 'Til Niagara Falls

I came across it as I was cleaning out some old book shelves recently. There among half-used up exercise books long discarded by various family members, some yellowed photographs and negatives too black and curled for recognition, it came tumbling down from some inner shelf recesses and fell flat on the floor – a small bound brown book, its pages tied to its cover with some ribbon. At first I was unable to remember what it was, but then gradually the light began to dawn.

It was my high school autograph book.

Autograph books! Do high school students in this more sophisticated age still take them around to friends for witty poems and pithy sayings? They existed in Australia during my girlhood, also in Ireland and Virginia while I was still a teenager, and it is interesting to see in the comments and poems of all three countries how similar are the entries.

Pithy maybe, but not always that witty though of course we thought them to be cat's pajamas. We rolled on the floor and were consumed with laughter over such gems as "Love many, trust few. Always paddle your own canoe," or "When you get married and have twins, don't come to me for safety pins." Well, I did not have twins, but my son did, and the need for safety pins had long since disappeared as the three-cornered pants gave way to the disposable diaper.

Then there were the short but "sincere" messages such as "To a swell girl, all the best," or "To a terrific team mate" or "To a fine camper" or the more dashing and clever (if somewhat cliche-ridden) signing-off words such as "Yours till kitchen sinks" or "Yours 'til the butter flies". These seemed hysterically funny once long ago.

How different our autograph books were, however, from those of the preceding generation. How flippant and foolish compared with the deep seriousness of the Edwardian youth of my father's day. His autograph book, which I still possess, is no small frivolous affair with pastel colored pages, but a fat exercise book with black shiny cover and, I believe, one put together for him when he left Australia as a Rhodes Scholar to go to Oxford.

I am fascinated by the art. If my own generation worshipped the George Petty girl – full bosom, long legs – to be found in the pages of Esquire magazine (read surreptitiously when adults were not around), his was the age of the Gibson Girl – full bosom, full hips beneath all those skirts, and hair piled up on top of the head. There are a couple of these girls, drawn in black ink, among the pages for my father's youthful delectation. My father once told me, in a slyly humorous manner, that in his days a young lady did not exist below the neck. I added nastily, of course, not between the ears either.

On one page, there is an elaborate water color painting done on stiff paper and pasted in, but for the most part, the entries consist of poems and comments of a serious "manly" nature, poems such as "And we'll all pull together," particularly appropriate for my father, a dedicated oarsman.

What struck me when I first came across this book, though, was the complete absence of humor or a lighter touch. After all, these were all young men of college age – there do not seem to be any entries by women – and it is hard to conceive that none of them had any less severe thoughts. One might think that even if they were never his 'til "the kitchen sinks" or "the butter flies", surely a poke in the ribs somewhere might have not come amiss.

Looking over my own autograph book of a generation later, perhaps someone might wonder if any of us ever had an interesting or intelligent comment to make. Or even an original one.

The Ads of Yesteryear

When, many years ago in Melbourne, Australia, a pharmaceutical company came out with a product called Gibb's Dentifrice – a tin of rather garish pink paste for cleaning teeth, I asked my mother if she would please buy some. The advertisements were so exciting. They depicted Giant Decay and tooth fairies battling against his evil ways and sent comics and gifts. Our usual tube of cream had nothing like that to offer.

My mother always said "yes" to all my requests, but, unfortunately, at this particular time, she was entertaining a friend who was less obliging and who promptly took over.

"You should never be taken in by advertising," she reprimanded me severely. "If a product is good, it doesn't need to advertise." What Madison Avenue would have made of that reply is interesting to conjecture.

Advertising was pretty simple in those days anyway. Large printed messages adorned the walls of the Melbourne streetcars which commanded "Men be like McAlphin's Flour. Always rise!" Most of the marketing suggestions then consisted of rosy-cheeked little children begging "Mummy, please buy some of that."

Growing up in America in later years, I became an avid consumer of women's magazines. With the arrival of Ladies Home Journal, McCalls or Good Housekeeping, I was lost in another world. Blissfully I sat down with each publication and read it lovingly page by page through until the end – stories, articles and advertising. As a result, samples of the last-mentioned usually appearing much the same with each issue, were engraved on my brain forever.

"She's lovely. She's engaged. She uses Pond's" read the exciting lines, each time above some gorgeous young woman. "Shocking says your hostess. Splendid says your dentist" was the message that went with a picture of a man hard at work gnawing on a monstrous bone that would help him to fight "pink toothbrush" – i.e. bleeding gums. Eminent physicians in white coats, stethoscopes dangling from their necks, told you to massage your gums – long before any Surgeon General's report had made itself manifest.

A favorite of mine, however, was always the advertisement for Sanka Coffee which showed, in a panel of pictures, Mr. Coffee-Nerves, a black and white ghost figure dressed in villainous top hat and tails, telling some husband or wife to stop taking so much guff from the other. The rude replies of the coffee-jangled spouse made for great fun reading. When, later, Sanka was discovered and Mr. Coffee Nerves made a hasty retreat, I hated to see him go. The happy reunited pair were so boring.

Other favorites appearing in like panels included the girl who had "hickies" and was thus never given a tumble but, on finding out about Fleischmann's Yeast, became the belle of the ball. And there was the poor little housewife whose husband very inconsiderately brought the boss home for dinner unannounced when the larder was bare. Almost. Happily she found a can of Franco-American Spaghetti lurking in its recesses, and the evening was saved. The boss complemented the wife on her cooking, and the husband was promised a raise.

All of these examples of advertising have long disappeared as the medium has become increasingly sophisticated, ruthless in its approach, and more hard-hitting. A quick glance through most women's periodicals these days can be almost completely exhausting.

English advertisements are, or were, when we lived there some years back, still relatively simple. "Somebody's Mum Doesn't Use Persil" showed kids eyeing a contemporary who was guilty of tattle-tale gray. The Bistro Kids have been smelling gravy now for half a century. My husband, always amused at the ads' simplicity, often cut out samples to save.

"When the fun gets fast and furious..." was one. It showed a silly looking elderly man in a paper hat and explained all this gaiety with a picture of Robinson's Lemon Barley Water.

"There goes Nurse Smith on another emergency…" was illustrated with a drawing of a couple peering nervously out the window as Nurse Smith set off down the street – on her bicycle.

Visiting France, we were enchanted with the pure artistry of their advertising though the message was often dubious. The one I remember most clearly was a drawing of the heads of three animals – a sheep, a pig and a cow. It was an advertisement for mustard, and each animal had a tear in the corner of its eye. "It will be used on us" was their promise. Enough to make one a vegetarian for life.

It pays to advertise obviously, or why would I, all these many years afterwards, remember all those catch lines and panels? The only thing is, however, I have never used any of the products. Perhaps because I never had pimples, pink toothbrush or coffee nerves. Or perhaps because I could never have put mustard on an animal with a tear in its eye.

To Age or Not To Age – That Is The Question

Recently, I directed a production of Robert McEnroe's "The Silver Whistle," a play in which a whimsical Pied Piper character brings the joy of life back to a group of depressed old people living in a rundown retirement home. "Life offers youth, but you insist on growing old," he tells them.

With these words still ringing in my ears I enrolled in a senior citizen driving course entitled "Mature Driving," a two-day session of reviewing the rules of the road most of us had encountered some 50 years ago, the purpose of which, to most of us, was to lower our car insurance rates.

"How has age affected your driving ability?" our workbook cheerfully queried and then went on to tell us – hearing impairment, vision loss, slowed down reactions, less ability to absorb alcohol – many such items that had never entered my mind heretofore. Many of the participants of the class began to sag visibly as we turned the pages.

"...to feel the wind and taste of Nature's wine, to smell the scent of her bouquet and listen for a drop of rain to fall and know for a moment, for an hour or forever, the haunting thrill of Nature's beauty, is to know the enchantment of the world. I say that be nine or ninety, these wonders should be ours."

So says the playwright through his leading protagonist, but "Mature Driving" said differently. Apparently we are unable in our senior years to either smell, see or hear anything very well anymore. And we were warned about the many drugs we depend on now, pills that cause drowsiness or elation when driving.

In "The Silver Whistle," however, the hero prods the old men back into life by giving them a secret potion –– in actuality rolled-up breadcrumbs – but it has the desired effect. He does not warn them about the dangers or drawbacks, nor does he worry as to how they will then conduct themselves as he works to bring back their lost self-confidence.

No such inspiration arose from "Mature Driving" which listed coldly and bluntly the limitations associated with aging in two relentless columns -- reduced (eye) pupil size, focusing ability (accommodative convergence), glare threshold and recovery, static visual acuity, central movement in depth, peripheral vision, color perception, glaucoma, cataracts, muscular degeneration, increased auditory threshold, organic heart disease, cardiac arrhythmias, hypertensive vascular disease, vascular aneurysms, arteriosclerosis, cerebral atherosclerosis, arthritis, cognitive limitations, osteoporosis, reduced motor transmission or reaction time. We also shrink in our old age so that the steering wheel becomes higher for us.

And, in case our spirits remain undaunted by all this, there is more, much more. We turn the pages of our workbooks, which with their simple pictures and diagrams are reminiscent of our children's reading readiness workbooks of yore, to see how one makes a left-hand turn, how to park, how to enter a highway, most of it a great deal simpler than the things we had to learn when we got our first licenses long ago.

Although none of us probably ever actually had to get out and crank a car to get it going, many of us remembered parents so doing. We did, however, have to learn the signals to be made with our left hand when driving, placing it out the window in a turned up position to show you were about to go right, in a straight position for left and down for stop. I memorized these easily as the three signs' beginning letters were RLS, the initials of my favorite writer, Robert Louis Stevenson.

We had to learn, too, to shift gears, to know how to let out the clutch slowly each time, often to work the windshield wiper by hand as we drove. Rainy weather meant getting out of your car also to fasten the flaps on the sides of your convertible. We tied luggage to the running boards either side of the car. The speed limit on the gauge was 60 miles per hour but no one ever went that fast – not on roads, even major highways – that were all two-lane.

"Look carefully for pedestrians when you are turning," warned our workbook, carefully illustrating such actions. "There is a lot of action going on at busy intersections." A real thought for the day!

Bad enough that we are supposedly so physically-impaired, according to them, but it is pretty obvious mental decay is at work, too. Tips for preparing a trip begin with "Know where you are going."

"Your minds are traitors to your hearts" the play's hero tells the old people, "telling you that you are weak, afraid and old. Your minds are lying to you."

"When unsure about a safe passing distance, do not pass," says the workbook as we are reminded also of our deteriorated state and, depressed, follow the text before us.

"What tragedy it is to see the dignity of man degraded by the loss of love for life," continues our Pied Piper character, "To shrink from life before the dust repays the dust from which it came is more evil that all the devil's sins incarnate..."

We need our poets sometimes even more than our guides to everyday living.

Onward and Upward With the Womanly Arts

When I accepted a position to teach English in an American private school for girls, I felt a tremendous sense of responsibility. Young girls should be instructed very carefully, not only in English, but in deportment and the womanly arts. I had been brought up on Louisa May Alcott. I knew.

First, deportment. A stint at the Pasadena Playhouse some years before had introduced me to the art of the stage faint.

"Fainting is very important," I told my girls. "One never knows when one might find oneself in a compromising position. Suppose a young man might offer an impertinence? Might even attempt to slip his arm about your waist?

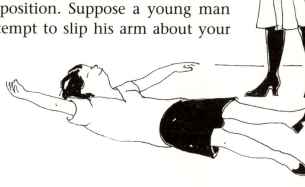

My girls shuddered at the thought. Almost fainted, in fact! Then, too, a proposal, or piece of shocking news, would certainly necessitate some sort of reaction in the fainting line....something, anyway, that called for *eau de cologne*.

So we practiced fainting! Not in class, of course, which was properly dedicated to literature, but at recess and lunch. The girls loved it. They fainted right and left and all over the place, none too gracefully, and often showing large sections of their gym bloomers. They could not wait to be offered impertinences. They fainted if they were late for gym or received a bad grade. A teacher speaking to any one of them in harsh tones elicited an immediate crumpling to the floor.

Reprimands went out and the fainting stopped, at least at school, although I often toyed with the idea of trying it myself in a faculty meeting.

The womanly arts were something else again. I was surprised, if not shocked to learn that my girls could neither sew nor knit.

They could do beadwork or make paper flowers, but that was the limit of their talents. In my Australian girlhood I had sewn my way through brush-and-comb bags, hair tidies, night-dress cases, though I had never achieved the crowning glory, the navy blue bloomer. We had also knitted large, and often long, face cloths from white string which became darker as the heat increased and more shapeless as our boredom grew.

Sewing in the classroom was out of the question. I did not think I could cope with the falling and rolling spools and scattered pins. But knitting was a nice, lady-like occupation, and in no time, I had my girls sitting around on lazy afternoons, their needles clicking as I read aloud to them from Jane Austen and Emily Bronte.

Their enthusiasm was boundless. They lugged their knitting out of English class and into every other class, ending up, unfortunately, in the science laboratory, where an enraged science teacher complained that her microscopes were being clogged up with hairs. I was summoned by the headmistress, and knitting ceased.

But still, many years later, I often run into my former students in stores and at parties, and they stand there beaming showing me the streaked and uneven sweaters that they knitted long ago in those memorable classes.

And we *both* faint for joy!

Fingering

Has anyone ever stopped for a moment to consider the tremendous significance of the finger? An anthropologist from the University of Chicago whose subject happens to be the fore limbs of the ape, has informed me that man is the only animal with the use of hands. Since monkeys use their front limbs to walk on, the hands or the fingers anyway, have never developed the way those of humans have.

But the finger comes in for attention all over, in expressions, literature and historical events. Aside from certain vulgar implications, it is the focus of a myriad emotions. To be officious and meddlesome is to have a finger in every pie. To be lazy is to be some one who will not lift a finger. To be inclined toward kleptomania is to be light-fingered or perhaps even sticky.-fingered. To have

complete control over another human being is to be able to wind them around your little finger and to be in real trouble is to have the finger of scorn pointed at you. To drop something is to be butter-fingered.

At elegant social functions we are treated to finger food, possibly slender dainty cakes known as Lady Fingers. Indeed in my youth, ladies themselves crooked their little fingers in mid-air as they held their teacups. Until it became known as vulgar to do so anyway. And as for eating daintily, those who indulge in the opposite are quick to remind you that fingers were made before forks.

"The moving finger writes and having writ..." wrote poet Omar Khayyam though one wonders how a single digit can be so facile all by itself. Those who unearthed the remains of Czar Nicholas II and in Russia came across, in perfect condition, a solitary finger. Anne Boleyn, mother of Elizabeth I of England had six fingers on one of her hands – the "better to suckle the devil's imps."

Remember the importance in Alfred Hitchcock's famous movie, "The Thirty-Nine Steps", of the man to watch out for – the man with a missing finger? A three-part TV movie shown last year of a kidnapping in Ireland had the kidnapped victim losing her finger as it was chopped off and sent to her husband as evidence. For good reason since there is no one alive in the world who has identical fingerprints. Their importance has caused many a miscreant to be discovered.

And who can possibly deny the importance of the third finger of the left hand?

Updating the Adjectives

Two of the more popular adjectives going the rounds these days, and most prevalent in those running for office, are *old-fashioned* and *home-made*. Both seemingly imply great virtue. Why?

<u>*Old-fashioned*</u> was, for many years, actually a term used in a derogatory sense. If your clothes were *old-fashioned*, they were considered dowdy. If your home decor was *old-fashioned*, you were behind the times, dated. And so were your ideas.

But suddenly *old-fashioned* became being superior and more worthy. The *"old-fashioned* values" were spoken of with deep respect and a touch of nostalgia by people deploring the modern ways of life and proudly claiming to adhere to ways of the past.

What *old-fashioned* values? History and literature give no visible signs of much in that direction. When I was growing up during the Second World War, I remember my mother coming to me and in a horrified whisper asking, "Girls today have gone about as <u>far</u> as they can go, haven't they?" Not being too sure of how far that was, I was unable to reply.

<u>She</u> could talk! She had been a young married woman during the Roaring Twenties and a young unmarried one during the Edwardian period, and we all know about the antics of the latter watching Channel 13 on TV. The monarch whose name was given to the period was not too much to applaud virtue-wise.

And before Edward, there was the Mauve Decade, that period of decadence notorious for producing Oscar Wilde and Aubrey Beardsley and their cohorts. Not too many *old-fashioned* values there to cheer about either. The Victorians kept up the stiff facade but behind it lurked much hanky-panky. The double standard was the value most observed by Victorian husbands. Those long weekend parties at England's more stately homes were divided by shooting all day and tiptoeing around the halls at night.

And so it goes – all the way back to Adam, Eve and their homicidal son who were evicted from the Garden of Eden. So where are the *old-fashioned* values so touted today? Perhaps they are values better eschewed than adopted?

And as for <u>*home-made*</u>! Before I begin to salivate over any *home-made* goodie, I would like to get a look at the home. My *home-made* clothes, self-produced for years, had long threads hanging down below. And they sagged badly. *Home-made* bread can be good if it rises to the occasion and cookies and cakes if the oven and the cook's memory are up to snuff. But so much of this can be touch-and-go that it is no surprise that many today rely instead on cake mixes and frozen entrees.

It is no use sighing for a past that never was. But if you still continue to yearn looking backwards, stop for a while and contemplate the plumbing.

Important Notice Delivered

The mail I receive daily leaves me in a perpetual state of wonder. It is so full of wonderful surprises, and they constantly provide me with much food for thought.

There is, for example, the letter that arrives regularly for my husband. It informs him that since he is a man of such high intelligence, such rare and sensitive taste, that he would no doubt be interested in their product. My husband would probably not be, but it is hard to tell. He died in 1981, having been almost completely incapacitated by a stroke since 1976.

At first, I found these letters very upsetting. Later, my more slap-happy side took over. Since each offer came accompanied by a self-addressed stamped envelope, I took to sending back a reply. I would carefully scrawl along the bottom of the page, deep thanks for the company's compliments, adding they were the nicest things he had heard since 1981 when he died. Or that he was glad that people still recognized these qualities in him since he had not been around for six or seven years. Or that the heavenly messenger had been kind enough to bring the offer by in the latest mail up above. I kept thinking of how much he would have enjoyed making up some of these answers which would, given his acknowledged intelligence and very real sense of humor, have been a lot cleverer.

Eventually, however, I began to realize that the letters had come from a machine and would go back to a machine, so it was all pretty hopeless.

When my husband died, my income took a steep plunge, and I cut my living expenses drastically. I was, however, constantly besieged with letters from credit companies offering me cards. I thought if they knew what I was living off, they would certainly change their tune. But since they continued to come, I ceased writing on each "deceased" and began to write "Mrs." in front of my husband's name on each one. In the space where I was to put income, I printed evasively, "retired." As a result, the cards poured in! American Express sent me a gold card.

I seldom use any of them, not wanting to run up debts I will be unable to pay. Today, however, I received an interesting billing for one never used. It stated under Minimum Payment Due "0.00." Under Past Amount Due, the same figures. Payment Due Date read 02/07/98 and New Balance 0.00. With this came a slip entitled in red, "Important Notice."

"Congratulations!" it read. "You've earned real money this year by using the _____ Card. Now we'd like to award that money to you. Just tell us how you want to receive it!"

And on the bill one is to read for instructions, "Qualified Purchases $0.00 Cashbook Bonus $0.00."

It is the easiest money I ever earned! With $0.00 I have got a lot of options.

Using It Up, Making It Do

I love to cook, and I am always excited when I wake up in the morning at the prospect of my next encounter with my kitchen.

Since I live alone, I am free to digress – though not always digest – any amount of experiments in the culinary line, the most challenging of all being the eternal leftovers lurking in the furthest recesses of my refrigerator.

Although I did not grow up in a Puritan household – making it do, using it up, and wearing it out, I simply cannot bring myself to throw anything out. The leftover green tomatoes on my vines in the fall become green tomato pickles, and pickles made from old watermelon rinds have inspired a poet and brought me fame.

I cannot pass up the challenge of producing something delectable from something unsightly unless it has actual hair growing out of it. My late husband usually found the results unsightly too but that has not deterred me.

Thus, one day last week when I dragged out a bag of very old potatoes from the back of my refrigerator and saw their wrinkled skin and unappetizing aspect, I felt my heart beating fast. Obviously, they could not be thrown out since their contents were still edible, but what to do with them? I began by boiling and then peeling them.

Then – an inspiration! Many years ago in Virginia, a black cook we had introduced my Irish mother to a southern recipe for potato rolls which from then on we ate every Sunday along with our fried chicken. Eagerly, I reached for my cookbook

and happily found a recipe for them under "refrigerator rolls". Fine, I thought. I could mix up the dough and store it in the freezer. I began happily putting yeast into warm water and set out a large bowl.

And a large bowl indeed was needed. I had, of course, not gotten around to checking out the amounts necessary of the ingredients that were to be used – only the ingredients themselves and since I had four cups of riced cold potatoes instead of the one called for, I had to quadruple every item that went into the bowl. Three eggs, for example, became twelve! One stick of margarine became four and a half cup of sugar became two whole cups.

The batter, now with added yeast, began to rise, bubble and overflow. I poured half of it into a large casserole cooking container, but the amount in both containers continued to grow in bulk. The kitchen sink was piled high with empty cartons, the flour bin was quickly emptied and I had to run out and buy more. And meanwhile, the great monster in the two bowls pulsated and heaved and reminded me of the mud volcanos in Yellowstone.

Glancing once more at the recipe book, I saw in an adjoining paragraph about refrigerator rolls that the dough cannot be frozen, and that if kept chilled, it would last only a few days. The advice was to cook before freezing. I turned on both upper and lower ovens.

Now I tried pouring out the contents of one bowl onto a floured surface, adding more and more flour as I tried to knead the still sticky batter. To my horror, I read the top line of the recipe which promised a yield of forty rolls. And I was going to have a hundred and sixteen! This was enough to cause a proper faint. However, instead, I pulled myself together, and I got out two bread pans, ladling as much as possible into each and putting both pans in the top oven. The rest of the dough I rolled out endlessly, shaping it into rolls and putting two trays at a time into my lower oven, removing each tray-load onto the counter before filling the tray up again. And in between cleaning up my kitchen.

Eventually, the kitchen was clean, the ovens no longer in use, and the bowls cleaned and put away and the counters covered with hot rolls and loaves of bread waiting to be frozen. I gave some to my next door neighbor. She pronounced them very good. I retired to my bedchamber.

All this to save a handful of aging potatoes!...

"Hose" Business Is It Anyway?

A close friend of mine now in her nineties (she makes me feel so young...) received a blow the other day when she set out to buy some more stockings. Stockings, she was told, no longer exist. What she really needed was panty hose.

Stockings no longer exist! But stockings are a great part of English literature. How can Malvolio in *Twelfth Night* appear in yellow ones, cross-gartered, and what are children with visions of sugar plums dancing in their heads going to hang up at the fireplace with care? But perhaps this might be the way people felt when girdles came in and garters went out, and goodness knows garters certainly played their part in history - *honi soit qui mal y pense* and all that.

My own early connections with stockings was with the long gray woolen ones that we wore to school in winter in Australia. These were held up by a device known as a "liberty bodice", a sort of sleeveless cotton jacket from which hung the essential suspenders and which we wore over our vests – or, as they are known in this country – undershirts. And when our stockings developed holes (usually in the knees), we carefully darned them and also any ladders – or runs – leading up to the holes.

Darning was really quite fun, so we quite enjoyed weaving the needle in and out and making a nice neat little patch, and I even knew of girls who purposely made holes in order to further their fun.

Here in the United States, however, when I turned up on colder days than we ever had in Melbourne, I was an object of derision. Stockings were just not worn here, I was informed as I stared at their bare legs now turning an interesting shade of blue. But, of course, I soon joined the throng...

And then there was that tantalizing glimpse of the first nylons on the market before they were quickly snatched up for the construction of parachutes during the war. In fact, during that time, the only stockings available were of lisle, nasty heavy unattractive creations so that quickly many of us turned to the bottle – liquid stockings, that is. Carefully we swathed our legs with this brown liquid, even more carefully did we draw slender lines down the backs of our legs to look like seams – no mean feat! All very well but when we got a mosquito bite or a scratch of some sort, chunks of white skin made their appearance, sometimes showing traces of blood as well. And as for swimming – well, our stockings were, alas, soon washed away.

Then the war ended and nylons were back in town – seamless stockings and panty girdles. Life seemed full of untold riches suddenly, so much so that a single run or ladder, merely caused the wearer to toss the offending article into the nearest trash basket. Panty hose were even better except that a run in one leg brought about the tossing out of both. But then the increased wearing of long pants among women made stockings and even panty hose less important in daily life.

So my ninety-year-old friend was unable to find the object of her quest, but since she lives in long pants anyway she can, no doubt, survive. But what is she going to hang up this Christmas with care and what is my son, John, going to go to bed with when he has no stockings on to take off? I doubt if he will turn to panty hose.

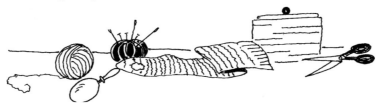

A New Life – WITH FUR

My cat, Tom, and I have lived by ourselves together for many years. We have long become accustomed to each other's peculiarities, each other's habits of eating and sleeping. He likes to sleep, actually, at the end of my bed in a massive lump, sometimes so humped up that I am unable to see the television screen at that end of the bed. I try moving him gently aside, but this only infuriates him and, after a brief pause, he once more claims his territory, humped up higher than ever.

Thus, recently I began to toy with the idea of bringing in some more youthful life to our house in order to liven us both up a bit – sort of like having another baby, a feat that neither Tom (who is fixed) nor I, who am old, is actually capable of producing. So I determined to adopt a kitten.

Really, it was like having a baby. I had to go out and buy another, and smaller, litterbox and a supply of Kitten Chow, to say nothing of a collection of bright new toys, though none of these last items seemed to catch the eye of Meg when I first brought her home from the barn in which she had first come to life. She at once rushed off and hid under the guest room bed, making only

tentative sallies from time to time. I spent the early mornings watching Princess Diana's funeral, eating my breakfast and holding Meg in my lap.This seemed to give her some assurance.It was not a barn, but it was warm and comfortable, and she enjoyed the leftover spoonfuls of cereal and milk.

But Time marches on and even a warm lap has its limitations. She began emerging from above on her own, sitting on the top of the stairs and looking about her, soon racing down in wild abandon as she became more sure of what was below. Tom, seated on his one end of the sofa, after an initial spitting, began to regard her philosophically, with a mild interest, before going back to sleep. I carefully arranged her litterbox and dishes in the downstairs bathroom, apart from Tom's in the kitchen, but in no time she was busily crunching away on his Mature Cats food, while he was working with some enthusiasm on her Kitten Chow. He even once used her litterbox, but I think it was because he was too lazy to make it down to the basement.

At first, Tom was too put out to continue sleeping at the end of my bed (the first time I had been able to see my favorite TV programs in ages). Meg rushed up to my bedroom nightly, however, with undisguised enthusiasm, purring so loudly the bed shook. Tom eventually returned, even sometimes emitting a rather toned down purr, or perhaps it was toned down compared to

Meg's. He settled once more at the end of my bed, forcing me to stick one of my legs on either side of his massive form – any slight nudge sending him stalking off in quiet rage. Meg has taken over my pillow on one side, purring away until around midnight when she decides that it is imperative that she get to work and do some vigorous washing. So vigorous that she often loses her balance and tumbles off the bed.

My normally neat living room is now littered with small tinkling balls, catnip mice and scraps of yarn, and much of my time is spent retrieving these objects, lying on the floor on my stomach and reaching under sofa and chairs. Meg's attention span is so short that she goes from one to another forgetting what she was doing just a minute ago.

She has indeed livened up our house, Tom and myself, bringing interest and amusement to us both. The first time I lit the fire this fall, she was flabbergasted, but soon became intrigued enough to come closer, settling down beside Tom on the hearth rug, creating a warm and charming picture of a happy home.

At the Perfect Age – If I Could Only Stay There

I had stopped at a traffic light and was sitting in my car, impatiently waiting for the light to turn green, when I saw them. A group of teenage girls in their usual garb of wrinkled jeans and slovenly tee shirts, their hair in the current messy mode, waiting for a school bus. Not even their clothes or hair could disguise their pretty young faces and slender, attractive bodies as they wriggled back and forth, chattering and giggling.

"You poor things," I murmured softly to myself, sighing with relief to be safe in my sixties.

I remembered when I had been that age – pretty, slim and perky, coming from a happy home, surrounded with loving friends and over-protective parents who gave in to almost every one of my demands.

And miserable.

Isn't everyone at sixteen?

Certainly no one ever told me then how wonderful it is to be old. Those were the days when one thought of being old as being over thirty, anyway. But the thought of turning grey or being alone or having to be careful about one's health would have appalled me had I ever given it a thought. But thinking is not a teenage sport in any case.

Given reasonably good health and enough income to live comfortably, the sixties are a very pleasant time of life, one of the most pleasant, in fact. So much of the strife and turmoil is over. The worry about what to do with one's life, whom to marry, where to live, how to manage one's children and, later, how to manage one's parents – that's all over and done with. And now that one has lived and been around sufficiently, one's like and dislikes have been sorted out and one is able to do more or less what one likes to do.

I missed my husband and children for many years, but the situation of living alone has become increasingly attractive. You can keep the house the way you like it, neat or messy – without annoyance if the former, without criticism if the latter. You eat what you like and when you like without having to put up with complaints; the books on the shelves are your choices, as are the pictures on the wall. When you feel lonely, you call up other people or throw a dinner party. If the guests are a married couple, you have the pleasure of talking to both of them instead of spending your evening with the wife while the husbands go off together in a corner.

Most satisfying of all in one's later years, however, is the fact that you are no longer upset about matters that once rocked you to your very foundations. Appearing at a social function in the wrong clothes, seeing a large pimple appear on your face the evening of a very important date, hearing someone make a joke about something you have said. In youth, any of these can be catastrophic. In old age, they are laughable. The nasty remark that turned you inside out in your more youthful times can now be regarded as a failing in the one who made it.

Once, in my younger years in America, unhappy over my "differences" and ashamed of my British parents who were unlike those of any of my friends, I came across a magazine article saying that when you meet people, you should not worry about what they think of you but of what you think of them. I have adhered to this gem of wisdom ever since. And as for my unusual

parents, I finally had the sense to realize that they were actually superior and to be proud of them.

And what a pleasure it is to be retired. No longer having to search for panty hose without holes, struggle into a girdle, or look for something appropriate for office or school wear. Best of all, no longer having to make the sometimes superhuman effort to get along with one's co-workers or to appease the unpredictable boss. No longer having to be excoriated or told off because of a failing of one kind or another – the sort of thing that can sometimes annihilate one for days. When my last job ended, I put the bottle of Maalox away forever.

It is a cliche to mention how wonderful grand-children are, but indeed they are one of the delights of old age. Well, too, there are many wonderful discounts these days for seniors, making it so much easier to attend museums and movies, ride on the train or in the limo to the airport, and pay for the doctor or the pills, sometimes even for home repairs. And thank God for Social Security!

A woman, whose husband employed me for many years, once said to me, "If I could just remain this age for the rest of my life, it would be so wonderful."

She was in her mid-seventies.

The Identical Me

I am an elderly woman
My hair is gray and my hands are wrinkled.
Yet I am the same person as the one that was
    the little girl playing on a swing in an Australian garden.
I am that same me.

I am the same me that traveled many times across oceans,
That rode in rickshaws in India,
That sailed through the Suez Canal,
That picked blackberries with my cousins in Ireland,
 I am that same me,
The one with the gray hair and wrinkled hands.

I am the same me that faced the hostile faces
Of my classmates in America
As they laughed at my strange accent and clothes.
That was me, too.
The same one that later skated with them on a nearby lake
And danced with them late at night to the sounds of a victrola.
Yes, that was me.
Now with gray hair and wrinkled hands.

That was me again in a London hospital
Holding my first-born in my arms.
Later another son born in Virginia,
Raised in a rowhouse in Brooklyn with a tiny garden.
That was the same me who is still here
The same one, the very same one.
Hard to believe.

The years have gone by fast and the sons are grown
With sons of their own,
But I am still. here, unchanged,
Except for the gray hair and wrinkled hands.

Where did the years go and why so fast?
With gray hair and wrinkled hands, I am still here unchanged.
I am that same me.

So many countries,
So many faces and accents,
So many different words and expressions,
So many homes and gardens and friends,
So many loved ones gone forever,
And yet I am still here.
The same me
The same me.
The one with gray hair and wrinkled hands.